Norbert Hirschhorn

Stone. Bread. Salt.

Poems

Holland Park Press London

Published by Holland Park Press 2018

Copyright © Norbert Hirschhorn 2018

First Edition

A CIP catalogue record for this book is available from The British Library.

ISBN 978-1-907320-76-7

Cover designed by Reactive Graphics

Printed and bound by
CPI Group (UK) Ltd, Croydon CR0 4YY

www.hollandparkpress.co.uk

In this very personal collection of poems Norbert Hirschhorn takes stock of his life and gives voice to his quest to pass on the experiences of the generations before him.

Norbert Hirschhorn experiments with rhyme and metre, free verse and prose poems, yet they all are in his inimitable voice, and together they tell a story.

This collection sweeps you along from London to New York and the Middle East and back again. At some points Hirschhorn almost literally stops readers in their tracks by using the + sign.

What makes this collection extra special is Norbert Hirschhorn's work on translating some of Fouad M. Fouad's poems from the Arabic.

Each poem can be savoured on its own but together they paint a picture of a thoughtful poet and American Health Hero (to quote Bill Clinton) trying to catch the essence of life to hand down to the next generations.

For Elisabeth, John and Robert, who have taught me about life.

BATHROOM SCALE
(After Rabbi Hillel the Elder)

I tell the truth.
Even if you stand on one foot.

Contents

PREFACE

In Judaism, the Hebrew word *tshuva* is a vital concept. It means *return*, but also *repentance*. It is said that God first created repentance, then the universe. Over the past decade I have made my own return: a journey to rediscover my Jewishness.

My parents and I had escaped from Vienna, one step ahead of the Nazis, to find safety in England, then America, but leaving my grandparents behind. An abiding, silent grief enveloped the family, confounding our Judaism, no longer a solace. Several years ago, however, my return began with the publication of *A Memorial Book*, telling the compelling stories of members of my Hirschhorn and Fischer families during the Shoah: those who survived and those who didn't. The stories were brought to light by letters and photographs kept faithfully by my uncles and cousins who knew they carried a history that must not be forgotten. Almost as a separate project, I returned to the language my grandparents and great grandparents spoke in my poetry collection, *To Sing Away the Darkest Days. Poems Reimagined from Yiddish Folksongs* (London, Holland Park Press, 2013). The history of the Jewish people in Europe can be heard in those songs.

In the summer of 2017 I traveled to Poland to see the killing fields and camps that almost destroyed all the Jews in Europe, but also was able to observe how some Jewish life has returned. On that journey, I discovered the mass graves where my grandmothers were buried, and there said the remembrance prayer. It is what humans need to do for their loved ones, whether they die peacefully in old age, with family gathered around, or anonymously at some killing field.

All lives are contingent, mine throughout: a narrow escape from Austria in 1938, stumbling into international public health, not being hit by any number of too-fast vehicles. It's been a charmed life – mistakes, tragedies and all. My career in medicine and public health allowed me to save many lives. My life saved permitted my children and grandchildren, and all coming after, to exist. I trace my own ancestors to the earliest time of life on earth, and before that to the stars. For this I stand in awe.

THREE SCORE AND TEN

My life: a Domesday Book,
a reckoning, deeds and misdeeds.

My life: the Encyclopaedia of Everything,
laid on its lectern open to the penultimate page.

Sometimes I wonder if I'm on some kind of
'Truman Show', me a solitary player

to whom, when it's over, that Audience
of One will offer a standing ovation.

I've misplaced my map – faded, smudged,
torn at the creases – where I'd marked a well,

fed by springs from an underground river. One sip
of those sweet waters, I thought, I'd be home free.

I keep her photo in my wallet.
When I collapse and die at the foot of a

Charing Cross escalator, people will
find it and say, *What a lucky guy.*

THE POET FANTASISES

living in a white-washed stone cottage,
on a Greek island, overlooking the Aegean Sea,
with the sound of goats' bells
clanking along the narrow dirt trail,
while a stooped crone (hairy mole on chin)
brings up salt cheese, fresh bread, olives, ouzo,
and just-plucked figs – so he'll be inspired
to write a poem about

living in a white-washed stone cottage,
on a Greek island, overlooking

ON REACHING SEVENTY-FIVE

I know Neil Diamond's 'Song Sung Blue'
(*everybody knows one*).

I know the Black Dog but not how to chain it.

I know the silken feel of backstroke in open waters –
land mass and horizon gone. Uterine.

I don't know the way: half-blind, stumbling
off a moonless trail.

I measure out my life in toilet rolls.

I knew two loyal creatures: Tippsie –
patient rug of a dog. Domino the Cat –
who refused to come in until we'd rubbed noses.

I held them in my arms as they died.

I know 'Unchained Melody'
(*Lonely rivers sigh, 'wait for me, wait for me'*)

I know I look good in a hat. There's comfort.

LIFE-COURSE DEPARTMENT STORE

entrance

   layette
   baby clothes
   teddy bears
      school back pack
      bike
      sneakers
         skateboard
         video games
         hooded sweats
            wedding list
            wine rack
            appliances
               gardening tools
               golf clubs
               treadmill
                  blood pressure cuff
                  optometrist
                  hearing aids
                     cane
                     walker
                     wheelchair
                        shroud

                        exit

LONDON WINTER BLUES

Long walk in the night   Sirens howl in two-pitch vibrato
+ a little child cannot stop crying   Dirty-diesel buses
growl past honking to get me out of the way   Someone
behind me keeps coughing   Home again   Cold night
air   sent out to shop at the 24-hour mini-market for
milk   Pakistani night shift workers   sleepy-eyed   scan
my stuff   don't help pack   I smile   what else

Rainy night   not much going on at home   walk to local
mall to suss out the bookshop   Closed   at 7pm   But the
cinema is thriving   bang-bang-shoot-em-up movies +
lots lots of places to eat + eat: Nandos   Rossopomodoro
Shikumen   Wagamama   Yo! Sushi   Yoo Moo Yoghurt
+ at the cinema all the popcorn/candy/supersize soda
pop to last a long long bang-bang-shoot-em-up   My
wife says she wishes she'd never got married   to anyone

On BBC website   black cloud icons every day for the next
five + counting   In Hawaii sunny   68°F + the surf is
up   Midnight here   a dirty mist descending   1°C   even
birds are coughing   My winter bronchitis has returned
+ I was escorted from a British Library reading room
when people complained

Hardly better in the morning   Worse   When I grew up
in WWII the pea-soupers so thick you couldn't see
your hands   People walked with canes   tapping the
pavement   If you followed the tail lights of an intrepid
vehicle you could end up in the driver's garage   I
survived air raids   buzz bombs   ambulance klaxons
bunkers   all-clears   smoke + fire

21

It continues dark + cold + drizzly   Outside the supermarket
the young homeless man with a scraggly beard sits
on a bit of newspaper   barely out of the rain under
the overhang   whingeing for money to be put into a
wrinkled styrofoam cup   On a piece of cardboard is
the sentence   neatly drawn by magic marker   Please
help   I'm hungry   What a time to be indifferent   I am
indifferent

Dark + overcast out   Cold   A few desultory flakes land +
die   Snow goddamnyou   man up   Then I think of
Aleppo   But it doesn't help   A stone in my shoe

False dawn   walk in my local park   I watch various breeds
of dogs running free + various breeds of humans
throwing balls from their 'dog ball throwing stick'
Jack Russell terriers are best   out in an instant + caught
on one bounce   A pair of long-nosed cadaverous dogs
on a single leash saunter by   muzzles grey   dark coats
they make me shiver   Whippets I ask   Yes + aren't they
beauties   Well   ya   sure + I give them wide berth   Lap
dogs   Pekes + Pugs looking like   yes here comes the
cliché   like their elderly women owners   The women
walk slowly   chatting in neighbourly fashion   the dogs
chatting in their own neighbourly fashion   nose to
backside   Come here often

Snow drops + a single crocus returning   like Persephone
sticking a toe outside   even if the sky is cold + grey +
still dark at 6:30 am   I distrust spring   a deceitful lover
demanding I be joyful promising beauty   immortality
It's winter I trust   when things are honestly dead
Cough   Cough   The crocuses don't care   they just do
their thing

Middle of the night rumination   Up in a clear sky hangs
    Jupiter   watchman of the night zircon bright   Spica in
    Virgo accompanying him over these past few months
    On these last days of February   the morning sky is
    scandalously blue   mocking me for still thinking dark
    grey thoughts   Never mind   life is

ENGLISH CUISINE
(English food isn't as bad as it tastes – Anon)

Bangers & Mash
Bubble & Squeak
Stargazy Pie
Spotted Dick

Kate & Sidney
Toad in the Hole
Dead Man's Arm
Gooseberry Fool

Fare for English children
Unaware they were poor
Sinking spoons in Kettle Broth
'Til our boys came home from war

Mushy Peas
Frog Spawn
Stinking Bishop
Stump

For Liz Taylor

In sequence: sausages and mashed potatoes; shallow-fried left over vegetables from a roast; pilchard heads baked into a egg-potato pie, staring out; suet pudding with dried currants; steak and kidney pie; sausages in pudding batter; suet pudding rolled up with jam; crushed gooseberries in whipped cream; cubes of near-charred bread made into soup; soaked marrowfat peas with salt and sugar; tapioca pudding; a smelly cheese washed in pear cider; root vegetable puree.

VILE JELLY

So cold in the operating theatre.
The nurse – her name tag 'Florence' –
draped my body in a thermal blanket:
    me, freezing in Crimea.

The surgeon drove a needle under
my eye, a numbing fluid,
Cornwall thumbing out Gloucester's
    vile jelly.

Strapped to the gurney, head held firm, ECG
leads on my chest and limbs, BP cuff
squeezing my arm like a python, IV drip
    delivering soporifics.

Twin lamps on the surgeon's magnifying
lens approached: my eyesight blurred,
a twilit fog. I became that deer
    traveling through the dark.

Water flushed my eye. Breakup of crystalline
light I'd seen before when as a child
I nearly drowned in a mountain lake,
    indifferent sun overhead.

Half-dream: suspended from the ceiling,
bathed in hydroponic fluid,
dozens like me in sterile glass tanks,
    asynchronous beeps portending disaster.

Clouded vision, peering through
    a rain forest spider web –
opaque lens sucked out, an acrylic
    immortal taking its place.

Later that night, my eye went blind:
    street lights from the window – blind;
fingers waving in front of my face – blind.
    'Deal with it in the morning.' I whispered,

as my beloved slept soundly beside me.

BECAUSE IT IS MY HEART AND
BECAUSE IT LIVES IN OUTER SPACE

I marvel at my heart, there,
buoyant against abiding darkness,

an egg-on-end cadent solitaire,
radiant with ivory clouds and ruby canals.

Yet, from time to time I see it pierced by
jagged jetsam, each shock making it

quiver alarmingly. I wish I could
reach up to appease its pain,

this fatal moon whose ache compels
what I've been afraid to guess –

past each new cycle around the sun:
later, colder, turbulence repressed.

After Stephen Crane, 'The Heart'.

Heart Sounds

1
From foetal life to my three score and ten,
three billion beats, and counting.
                           Brave mass
of muscle, no larger than my fist,

uncomplaining, day and night –
                          no servant
or slave so loyal, yet ruling me, its master,
for without its fidelity my brain

would turn to mush in minutes.
                      Its metres are poetic:
lubb dup   lubb dup   lubb dup in iambic –
knowing too when to pound out a lover's delight

or to rush for a train. If ever in failure
it can be saved: Withering's dulcet foxglove
                      or Big Pharma's

angiotensinconvertingenzymeinhibitor.

2
There are days when 'heartache' is more than grief
when spasm seizes the left side of my chest
making me hesitate to speak   Did it radiate
Or was that just a sore elbow   Was I short of breath
Or hyperventilating Those skipped beats oh dear cardiac
    arrhythmia

Maybe just a panic attack

28

I imagine the real event happening   Whom would I call
      Where is my wife
Would I just sit on the front steps waiting for the ambulance
      to come
Passersby staring   Can anyone do CPR?   How embarrassing
      if
the electrocardiogram was normal   Or would I prefer a
      real heart attack
I don't want to die   How would the New York Times
      obituary read
If there is one   It hasn't happened   Yet

3
                  Three am, Boston City Hospital,
yet another admission: *Elderly black*
female, obese, short of breath.

I pushed aside her breast to *auscultate*
her heart: *lubb dup   lubb dup   lubb...*
            I woke with a start, my head on her chest,

mortified. She simply smiled and said,
'That's alright doctor, you needed your rest.'
            I hear you calling, dear heart.

JUNE 8, 2038

I died on my one hundredth birthday.
King Harry's Birthday Greeting
got lost in the hospice mailroom.

I wonder if I made the Guardian.
No one down here knows.

Actually, an ordinary day.
Early light woke me.
A blackbird carolled variations.

Roses on my bed tray.
Balloons on the ceiling.
Someone shaving me.

I don't need to pee.
I still had all my teeth.

That chocolate ice-cream
tasted good to me.

I never made anyone cry.
I just want to sleep.

DIRECTIVES FOR MY FUNERAL
(...makes death seem the happiest thing to happen
– Derek Walcott)

Wrap me in a shroud of white linen,
lower me straight into the ground,
throw down soil from the Holy Land.

Hold three memorial celebrations:
With Fairuz in Beirut carolling *kisses to the sea*,
Janet Baker in Britain singing Elgar's angelic

Where Corals Lie, and Patti Smith in America,
with *A Hard Rain's a-Gonna Fall* (you'll cry).

Serve enough food so anyone can come,
whether in jeans and tees or tux and gown –
And dancing!

*

I can't be with you, ageless yet impervious
to customs and time, so putting you under
no obligation, joyous as such moments would be.

Recently I spoke with my ancestors
Oh, what did they say?
They said my only obligation is to be a good ancestor.

ODE TO MY OLD PASSPORT WALLET

My beloved bought me a new one
(good heavens!) to replace my *Genuine Morocco*,
the one embossed with gold-stamped pockets
evoking a less fevered time: *Railroad Ticket*,
Baggage Check, Cabin Card.

There I kept a taped-up yellow booklet –
International Certificates of Vaccination –
revealing my homes with a previous
wife, anti-rabies shots that nearly took my life,
smallpox boosters against virus inhaled
from pustular patients in Bangladesh,
cholera, typhoid, diphtheria
(which hardly anyone spells correctly).

In another pocket, my now expired passport,
its many-hued stamps (Bhutan's the loveliest),
entry visas, exit visas, scribbles by border police
from six continents.
                    No, whither I go,
so goeth my passport wallet, to that place
where the only visa needed is a *broken and
contrite heart*.* Its body now like mine:
creased, cracked, worn, torn; skin tags
from a long-dead goat hand-tanned
by a man despised for his trade.

*Psalm 51:17

My Friend the Scholar Comes at Last to Attend His Father

He considered the wasted body lying there, moult
Of a once ferocious man, the mouth agape, muscles

Twitching with every rattled breath. *Agape* –

My friend the scholar reflected on the homograph,
Marvelling at the thing that feasted on his father.

He laid a futon at the foot of the high, white

Hospital bed; some books, a laptop, travel mug.
Nearby: an emesis basin, dentures, enamelled

Bedpan, a glass half-full of beaded water.

Sliding a hand inside his father's hand, he felt it
Grip back reflexly – a hand he remembered from
     childhood,

One he could find in any clutch of strangers, find in the
     dark.

He murmured to his father in their shared *ur*-language,
The way mourners linger at a grave to catch

The dead up on news, or beg release, as he stroked

His father's limbs with lotion and powder.
Vitriol would be more apt, he thought, to commemorate

The rage that seared them together.

His father was dying, absurdly beneath balloons and
   flowers,
And he felt that mute bewilderment of savanna
   elephants,

Swaying in a makeshift circle around one of theirs.

EVEN IF HE CAN'T ANSWER
MAYBE HE CAN HEAR YOU

Worst head trauma I've seen since Vietnam
said the neurosurgeon.
Some troubled kid had tossed a football-sized rock
from an overhead bridge through the car window
and my father caught it, perfectly.

In coma for months before
the pneumonia caught him.

The nurses urged me to talk to him
Maybe it will help to heal his brain –
as they went about changing his sheets.

His hand grasped mine (*primitive reflex*, they said)
either to trite or loving words I called up:
Hi Pop, it's me, your son, can you hear me?
Can you hear me?

The nurses urged me to talk to him. Sure,
shout down a high canyon, a fogged-in abyss.

I wasn't a grieving widow speaking
into a gravestone; we had little to say
even when he was alive.
I wished him dead, get on with my life.

For a year after, I couldn't drive on highways.
Now, at his age, I talk to him in my head.

SALOMÉ WITH THE HEAD OF ST. JOHN THE BAPTIST

I, Michelangelo Merisi –
known in my time and yours as
    Caravaggio
painted this scummy episode:

a pouty nymphet who made
stepdad Herod come in his pants,
now refusing to look at the
head-on-a-platter,

and besides it was all my
stupid mother's fault.

You might think instead this was –
    as you people say –
about 'speaking truth to power'
and look where it gets you.

No, for me, the really compelling
character is the executioner: jug-eared,
busted nose, A kind of in-your-face self-portrait.

the sort of thug you'd hire off the docks
to do some dirty work and do it right.

THE PIGEON CHASER

whirls a white cord
to stir his birds from their roost.

They rise and spiral, tangling with other flocks
in mock combat, upwards and sinking in synchrony.

No person knows in which country the end will come.
When the stones speak, what will they say?

When you aren't beside me are you there at all?
You wink in, you wink out of my hours.

A violinist plays a Bach partita in a hospice corridor.
Patients in coma blink, stir.

Only the roads know where to go.

SYRIA, 2017

Look, Damascus will cease to be a city,
will become a heap of ruins (Isaiah 17:1)

Death begets rebirth
Your acolytes shall inherit the earth
Beelzebub your host of flies
Drink tears from babies' eyes
Carry shit from drainage ditches
Dysentery and scabrous itch
Flies that feed – black   carrion   horse
Flies on shrouds on bridal corpse
Midges piercing gauzy mesh
Botfly maggots in festering flesh
Drones that buzz before you die
O! Loathsome Lord of Flies

The Disappeared

What makes us human is soil.
Landfill of bones, shredded tees, jeans;
mass graves paved over for parking.

What makes us human are portraits
– graduation, weddings –
mounted in house shrines and on fliers, *Have You Seen?*

Names inscribed around memorial pools,
and incised on granite. Names waiting,
waiting for that slice of DNA, any piece of flesh,
to be buried along with grief.

What makes us human is soil.
To stare into a hole in the ground,
fill with the deceased, throw earth down,
place a stone. Bread. Salt.

For Fouad M. Fouad

SHMITA

This is the year of the Shmita.
To violate the Shmita would be like
Eating your children.

Not in-your-face yiddish, but Hebrew –
Leviticus – meaning 'release'. Every seventh
Year the land is returned to rest. No ploughing,
No planting, no pruning, no harvest.

Barley, oats, millet, rye to be drawn from stocks,
And fruit off trees even the poor may crop.
The fig is prized, Eden's Tree of Knowledge,
So that we too may ripen to wisdom.

Shmita: temperance, rest from gain and need:
A respite from debt, ease bestowed on those
In distress, the dispossessed. All slaves freed.

KILLERS LIVE LONG

1.
They have time to water their plants in their gardens,
and once in a while go to the theatre.
When necessary, they replace old dentures
with new ones fit for biting.
Elderly killers,
their bones rattle while jogging the seashore.
Ribbons of blood dribble behind them
like a crippled dog.

2.
Killers mince cured meat with a kitchen knife
and lick the tang of salt left on their fingers.
'White tiles'
is how I describe their kitchens.
'Salt'
is how the killers
preserve their memories.

3.
The street is potholed by knees.
Blind sounds echo off walls.
What was once an arm is now a rope.
The corpse across the road belongs to no one,
not even to One-Eye on the roof
who stitches up rag dolls,
leaving puddles of blood clotting on Nikes.

By Fouad M. Fouad. Translated from the Arabic with the poet.

After the Barrel Bomb

A headless doll –
wrenched off at the neck
like a fetish
a witch sticks pins into

No No No
that's my child, not some rag doll
with its eyes gouged out
not a piece of junk
tossed into the rubble

she just had a haircut   see
to get ready for school
her lace dress
and little beaded earrings

where are those earrings   where
she had such rosy cheeks
I pinched every morning
after her bath
and her baby teeth
three came out last week

No No No
my baby wasn't some moppet
to be beheaded by that witch –
oh God how did my child
deserve this evil
oh God why does this acid
bite into my flesh

my headless child
she wasn't a floppy puppet
when she reached out her arms
to hug me
now her arms are stretched out
but never ever to hold me

headless child   headless child   headless

By Fouad M. Fouad. Translated from the Arabic with the poet.

Lost at Magnetic North

not quite true north
hidden in a valley

frozen   sunless

aimless place   a copse
immured in time

smokeless stone-hut chimneys

perhaps the men went hunting
solitary crack of a shotgun   or

crash of a tree limb

safer to be at some *ultima thule*
hubbub   jollity   light

a dog howls dumbly in the hollow

Canon Lens 18-300 mm

Perhaps a time to water plants growing
by a fallen wall, a shattered alley
in the black-and-white city named Aleppo.

In the gap between two houses, a sparrow
trembles in a child's hand, and a fighter
combs his pomaded hair behind a stack

of books shielding against death from the sky.
Inside the church an angel, wings outstretched,
pierced by tears and bullets, and a boy

smutched with dust, laughing. The fighter sucks
seeds from a pomegranate, lets his rifle
rest against a wall. In Aleppo.

In Aleppo, Death grows in alleys like a
rotted plant, pours from the sky:
nuts, bolts, TNT and chlorine.

People on bread lines know all this.
Also children reciting in school.
And a hunchbacked old man.

*By Fouad M. Fouad. Translated from the Arabic with the
poet. Written as an introduction to a photo exhibit 'Alep
Point Zero', by Mozaffer Salman, Paris, May 2015.*

The Wolf in the Hospital Corridor

Lurking in the hallways
Like a revenant creature
Where antiseptics fail
And visitors pass by
Heads hung low

Bandages unroll in the waiting room
Following drops of blood
Patients poisoned by witchcraft
Rancid fat on the beds

The wolf in the corridor
Its spectre on the wall
Racks the little girl
And her grandmother

Don't rest your head on that foul sheet
Don't ask the woman behind the door
Why she is crying

The wolf in the corridor
Put down the oud
Choke off the singer
We all are dying

By Fouad M. Fouad. Translated from the Arabic with the poet.

THE LAST NEANDERTHAL

The gold ball sinks into the sea
I hum in my throat
It grows cold

I liked keeping warm with my woman
Skin to skin
A fire in front of the cave

We were full
Food from shells the great-winged birds
Smashed on the cliffs below

Eggs from their nests
Nut grass   fallen-fruit   roots
Meat when our spears took flight

I like making noise
From both ends of my body
It grows cold

When the long legs came
They threw my children into the fire
They took my woman

The Wall Artist of Aleppo

No end. I wake to a rain of nuts + bolts
+ stink of diesel. I go to sleep by
candle light + crackling roar of a building's
collapse next door. I dream a digital dial
counting the dead, spinning faster + faster.
By day I paste manifestos on
remaining walls, scrawl poems + curses.
Nearly nothing left to eat.

I say what I want + say what I don't want.
I want to shake the world by its shoulders –
it's like touching a shade, a hologram.

I read in my holy book the myth of
resurrection, while barrels from the sky
feed real people, our mouths wide open.

Based on a poem in Arabic by Fouad M. Fouad.

LEBANON MON AMOUR

Because the man in his BMW stops at the crosswalk and
  waves,
  Welcome, go ahead, I won't hit you

Because young people call me Uncle, *Ya Am*

Because of Civil War warlords and bullet-pocked buildings
  – still here

Because of two hundred thousand dead, twenty thousand
  missing

Because Abu Ali, over eighty-five, harvests trash in his
  ancient truck –
  Where are my children?

Because of mezze, mouneh, tabouleh, mujaddara,
  mankoushe, kibbe, and arak
  teslam edayk – bless your hands

Because the electric company's neon signs are out

Because friends worry if I look sad although they have
  more reason

Because the muezzin's first call echoes through my dream
  –
  come to prayer, come to salvation

Because soldiers on guard fiddle with smart phones

Because fierce-looking bearded men cuddle infants to
their chests

Because a woman in veil and long coat walks beside a
stunner in stilettos

Because loving Lebanon is like swimming in honey

Because each time I leave she won't leave me

ENFOLDED BY FLOWERS

The *Star of Jerusalem*'s attar
floats through our bedroom,
                lasting 'til dawn.

You pin a *Gardenia*
to your flowing black hair.
             Five-petaled *Frangipani*,

pungent spoor of a goddess:
Yes, if worn over the left ear,
Perhaps, over the right.
               Jasmine crowds

the trellis on the long passage
to your house,
incense overwhelms night, a full moon.

           After the *Tuberose*,

morning lips swollen with kisses.

BOUND UP IN THE BOND OF LIFE
(*i.m. Johanna Hirschhorn-Navrey*, 1910-2005)

My enchantress Aunt Hania loved being in love.
Said no to the rich Austrian leaving for New York.
Said no to her sisters off to Palestine.
Said yes to Jack: Jewish, German, journalist,
Communist. *1935*. They fled to Russia.

Two years later: Jack arrested, exiled
to Siberia, died. Perestroika: my cousin Ruth
unearthed NKVD files, and read:
Ne vinovny – Not guilty.

When Jack was transported by train, he tossed
a crumpled scrap out the barred window
with only an address and a note:
Take care of little Ruth. A helpless
angel saw the message fly; retrieved it,
went to Moscow, delivered it –
hard labor or worse if caught.

War. Nazis at the gates. Young,
pretty, fearless, Hania charmed their way
on to a train evacuating wounded troops
to Kazakhstan, where she met Ruvim:
Russian, soldier, Jew.
Gentle Ruvim, simple Ruvim, raised Ruth as his own.
Years later Hania said, *I never
quite loved him.*

1945. Ten-days back by train, a side-track
where she jumped off to collect hot engine water
for bathing, tea, when a Polish Jew repairing rails
looked up and recognised his cousin. They
hugged, kissed and hugged, *but*
tell no one, please, not yet. After
Stalin died, only then he posted a letter
to *Kol Yisroel* whose daily radio
summoning of survivors called out:
If Erna or Lusia Hirschhorn are still
alive, please write, your sister lives.

America, *1956.* We got the blue air-letter,
Cut this flap first, which my father tore
and began to sob, *My sister's alive, my sister's*
alive. I'd never seen him cry.
Bound up in the bond of life.

1999. Hania returned to Germany, come to rest
in a nursing home: near-blind, bed-ridden, hair straggled,
haggard. *Hab mich verändert?* Have I changed,
she asked. *Ein bißchen*, a little,
I replied. She smiled at the irony.
Lebensmüde, tired of life,
she sighed, yet still
sang-spoke for me the old Resistance song,

Die Gedanken sind frei
wer kann sie erraten
Sie fliegen vorbei
wie nächtliche Schatten*

Like nighttime shadows.

53

*Our thoughts are free,
who can discern them?
They slip by, like
nighttime shadows.

The Princess & the Doula

Once upon a time there was a Princess who thought she
was a turkey. She refused to dress, walked with a
waddle, spoke with a gobble. She hid beneath the royal
tables, pecking at fallen food. The King, desperate,
promised the hand of his daughter to any man in the
realm who could heal her. Many tried, none succeeded
(charms, chains, potions, incantations). One day, a
doula – birth companion – came into town; someone
used to hard life, sorrow, but also joy. She saw the
broadside in the market & thought she could, at least,
offer comfort. The King's viziers laughed, slapped
their thighs, but the Queen said, *Let her try, we have
nothing to lose.*

Rather than interrogating the Princess about her childhood,
or shouting at her to stop being silly, the doula simply
undressed, crawled under the table & began to peck
at the crumbs. After some days, the Princess asked
the doula, *Who are you?* To which she replied, *I am a
turkey.* The Princess, surprised, replied that she, too,
was a turkey. They continued to forage together. After
some weeks, the doula told the Princess, *You know,
we can still be turkeys but turkeys who wear clothing,*
& put on a shift. The Princess, astonished, agreed to
a chemise, later slippers, eventually her gown. She
returned to the tables of the Royal House, but whenever
she wanted she could still be a turkey, just like before.
The doula went on her way, just like before.

Adapted from a story told by Rebbe Nachman of Bratzlav.

The Destined One

(*Two roads diverged in a yellow wood...
and I – I took the one less traveled by...*
– Robert Frost)

And I, I escaped from Vienna to London – the War –
then Manhattan where I grew up, became a doctor,
marrying M, a Catholic, which made my parents cry.
Yearning to cure the world, I flew to Egypt, divorced, met
    C –
an anthropologist – fell in love: this the one true road I've
    traveled.

And I escaped from Vienna to Palestine where I grew up,
became a GP. Yearning to heal the world I practiced
in the Negev, met C – an anthropologist studying Bedouin
    traditions –
fell in love, joining the road I've traveled.

Escaped from Vienna, but not New York or Palestine,
grew up in London, a GP, married my classmate's
sister E. Our careers estranged us. Yearning
to restore my world I turned to public health, met C –
a professor teaching Bedouin culture – fell in love,
crossing against the light.

Instead of M, Catholic, I married a cousin's friend N,
whose warm, Jewish family nestled me into suburban
    medicine:
big house, big pool, Cadillac DeVille; made my parents
    proud.
When N grew morose, I starved. Yearning to escape my
    world,
I just walked away, turning to public health, where I met
C, my Pole Star, on the only road I've traveled by.

For Cynthia

THE POLLARD

Whenever I'd ask for a game or toy
my father said, 'Money doesn't grow on trees.'
'What do trees have to do with me?' I sassed.

He drew for me our family tree:

How my great grandfather thrashed winter flax
for a pitiful living in the shtetl –
murdered by Cossacks.

By the rivers of Babylon there we sat and wept.

How his son – a scribe, a poet – for whom I'm named,
died of TB when the family fled the Great War.

How the widow raised five children by herself,
sewing clothes for Viennese parvenus,
surviving until the Nazis closed in.

How I, my son, escaped – now come to tell you.

SELF-PORTRAIT

My parents prayed I'd learn what it meant to be Jewish –
the Rabbi discerned I lacked the mien to be Jewish.

I hated *shul*, I longed for pork. Growing up in New York
with skull caps and spittle, I felt demeaned to be Jewish

and fled to the Ivy League: bell-bottoms, button-downs,
gentile girls and beer. By no means would I be Jewish,

a race that runs together, exposed by vicious words –
grub, wonk, wej, (with money, *mean*) – as being Jewish.

If we were little Davids, they might pat us on the head.
Goliath in Gaza? Rabid! mean! being Jewish.

Despite my conversion, I was still scorned. *But*, I cried,
it's the way I was born. I didn't mean to be Jewish.

Then both my parents died. I couldn't decide if, when, how
to say *kaddish* – I'd lost the means of feeling Jewish.

I went to a Wise Woman – elderly, with bright eyes –
and asked her straight out; what does it mean to be Jewish?

We're a people with history. We're your passport
to the past. History! No mean thing, being Jewish.

The best of us rebelled, the worst compelled by passion.
You're not average (mode, median or mean) being Jewish.

That other stuff you know – learning, charity, justice –
just don't forget to laugh at yourself. By all means, be
*   Jewish.*

My original name was Nathan. It means in Hebrew, *given*.
You are what you're born with. I mean to be Jewish.

The Penitent

Answer me.
A blind minstrel, wandering the wilderness
descends a valley with his kitara
made of boxwood, wanting for consolation.
                    Let the great
horned owl keep its eyes perpetually
open, an emptiness staring
in, an emptiness staring out.
        Answer me.

For I am wanting. Paper scraps
in my pocket: Buy eggs, milk,
honey, kiss the kids. I am
good enough.
                    Where goes my life?
No answer comes. I will not ask.
No lists, no pleas, no promises, no apologies.

The ram's horn sounds a Jericho blast.
Save me.

i.m. Dannie Abse

A Continuous Life

the man is swinging a hammer
he's hammering a lost-head nail
he's joining one piece of wood to another
he's building a floor with his own hands

    a house he is building
    shelter for his family
    being good husband and father
    his whole life as a 'good person'

    his whole life passed as 'a good person'
    good husband and father
    sheltering his family
    in a house built by his own craft

he built a floor   handily
he joined pieces of wood
he hammered the nails
he swung the hammer

WALLS

Mother said if I felt bored to bang my head
against the wall, it would feel so good when I stopped.

Wall to wall scoldings.
She said I drove her up the wall with my whining.

Mother and I, both off the wall.
The fly on the wall tried to escape.

When she was dying she did what was called for –
turned and faced the wall.

Interrupted Journey

A ritual we play
on each separation –

at a departure gate, say.

I wait, she waits.
I wave, she waves again and again

until one of us is out of sight.

We play at this rehearsal,
but like seeing someone hit by a truck –

until *you're* hit, impossible to know.

Left to our saddest imagination,
perhaps we'll hold hands

when they put us on a train.

Beirut Aubade

Thunderstorms bleached
    the pre-dawn sky – by morning
  the swollen sea boiled with whitecaps, seagulls'
       wings flickering in the sun, while terns
    savaged fish
whipped to the surface.
      On shore, the stink of burning trash.

A Nation Sundered

The leaders are waxen fat, they shine: yea, they overpass the deeds of the wicked: they judge not the cause, the cause of the fatherless, yet they prosper; and the right of the needy do they not judge. (*Jeremiah 5:28*)

For the rich men thereof are full of violence, and the inhabitants thereof have spoken lies, and their tongue is deceitful in their mouth. (*Micah 6:12*)

Because you have plundered many nations, all the remnant of the peoples shall plunder you. (*Habakkuk 2:8*)

Are you better than Thebes that sat by the Nile, with water around her, her rampart a sea, and water her wall? (*Nahum 3:8*)

Destruction upon destruction is cried; for the whole land is spoiled; suddenly my tents are laid waste, my shelters in a moment. (*Jeremiah 4:20*)

'Nobody reads the Bible more than me.' (*Donald J. Trump 24:2, 2016*)

CAT MEETS RAT IN NEW YORK ALLEY

Feral Cat corners Norway Rat
who pleads, *Don't eat me,*
I survived North Tower's collapse.
'No skin off my teeth, or claws,
I'm hungry,' says Cat. *But I taste awful –*
sodden pizza, dumpster offal,
not your kind of meal. 'Pizza, you say?
With pepperoni? Yum! Make my day.'
Please don't eat me, I've got brothers,
sisters, cousins, children, mothers,
all who depend on me.
'Welfare crap, I'm a Libertarian Cat, free
to eat what, where, and when I please.
You're morning's pie, so quit the shtick.'
Then here's my neck, please be quick.

No sooner said, Cat preparing to dine,
when Norway Rat sucked out his eye.

Based loosely on Aesop's Fable, The Cat and the Cock.

CHRISTIAN CO-WORKERS SCHEDULE
AN IMPORTANT CONFERENCE ON YOM KIPPUR

Would they notice if I wore a yellow star?
Would they hide me then? Or turn in my name?
Better not ask, mustn't push my friends too far.

'Come in, come in, have bread, have tea. Look, a jar
of honey even. I'll be right back,' he claims –
of course, *he* saw that I wear a yellow star.

Israels and Sarahs* in a railroad car:
trembling, bewildered, they are afraid
even to ask. And don't push friends too far

to look at your forearm, or examine your scar:
cancer survivors feel the shame
when radiation leaves a yellow star.

That ugly word for twilight: *crepuscular*,
like *kike* or *zid*, *hebe* or *sheeny*, shady all the same.
Don't ask your friends what their meanings are.

Don't ask your friends what their leanings are:
stir up trouble, you'll be blamed.
You cannot, must not, push your friends too far,
or they'll make you wear the yellow star.

*In 1938 Nazi Law #174 forced all German and Austrian
Jews to take middle names: Israel for men, Sarah for
women.*

LAMENTATIONS

On that night of crystal traceries
we listened for whispered news
of ones we sought: no news, no trace,
disappeared from the news.

Listen! Wisps of hourly news:
Is the news true? A truce?
Those images disappeared from the news
just as we prayed for a truce.

How our hopes depended on a truce
in our whispered, else wise traceless
prayers for news of a truce;
leaving us bruised, traces

of wounds otherwise traceless.
We prayed for a truce,
but God's bruising silence left its trace,
fracturing all hope for the truce

we'd prayed for. The news
on that night of crystal traceries
fractured hope with prophetic news:
No truce, no news, no trace.

LETTERS FROM VIENNA
(1938-1941)

Did we know what was going to happen?
Our children in America won't let us starve.
Not a single child with us, scattered all over the world.
If I could pour out my heart to you on paper I could write
    whole books.
You read the newspapers so you know everything.
What's your news? You shouldn't be too much in the sun.
By us is as by old people.

As if I'm looking over my grandparents' shoulders,
sitting at their deal kitchen table as they write, but
I'm the only one there who knows what will happen.

Repair Begins with Confusion*

Creation was a calamity. At the Big Bang,
a radiance without end burst into numberless fragments,
sparks descending to earth, penetrating
every living thing; each ember solitary, flickering,
urgent to rejoin into a beautiful flame.

Tikkun – healing, restoration. So, care for yourself,
care for the one who has wronged you,
care for the world about you.
But why did you need to know about the sparks?

There were actually two trees in Eden: the Tree of
    Knowledge
of Good and Evil, and the Tree of Immortal Life.
As a child I wondered why Adam and Eve didn't first eat
from the Tree of Life, and only then, Knowledge!
They'd live forever, knowing everything.

That's just it, they didn't know. Yet how I came to exist:
a result of ignorance, whose ways I continue to follow.

Repair begins with confusion.

***

Chase after Fame, she eludes you. If you flee,
she pursues – unless you peek over your shoulder
to see if she still follows; even in old age.

Am I good? How good?
If I give money to this homeless person
shivering on the pavement, maybe it's for self esteem:
I'm the kind of man who gives money
to this homeless person shivering on the pavement.

Or, maybe *If I give money to this homeless person*
shivering on the pavement, my companion will smile,
squeeze my hand.

Or, because it is a 'street tax':
Good fortune has entrusted me with this money,
to give to this homeless person, shivering on the pavement.

It is said the Jewish philosopher Rabbi Moses ben Maimon
    (Maimonides)
wrote an answer first, then filled in the question.

Don't try to be good, it only confuses.
Menachem Mendel of Kotzk, said when the Evil One
wants to destroy us, it won't be through our wicked desires
but through our wanting to be good. We do good at the
    wrong time,
with the wrong intentions, and end up doing harm. Yes.

Perfection is unattainable, an obstacle to humility.

The Kotzker Rebbe once asked some learned men, *Where*
    does God live?
The men, surprised, replied, *Why God lives everywhere,*
    and throughout.
No, he lives wherever we let him in.
The way each of us stands at the centre of a rainbow,
so we each stand at the centre of creation,
and must behave accordingly.

***

Eden's serpent was cursed with dust and dung,
the way God encumbers the rich with wealth.
Only the poor can afford to be generous.

I snubbed the Roma woman selling 'The Big Issue', after
    which
I fell off a ladder.
To shame someone is a grievous sin.

A Hasid once taught, When is it permissible to deny God?
When someone needy comes to you, don't say,
God will provide. By denying His existence,
you must provide.

***

An old man complained to his rabbi that his children
wouldn't have anything to do with him. The rabbi threw
    up his hands,
*That's how it is. How is it one father can take care of ten
    children,*
but ten children can't take care of one father?

Someone played a trick on Mother Hen, put duck eggs in
    her nest.
Brooded and hatched, the ducklings took off for the pond.
Come back darlings, you'll drown! –
Don't worry, mother, we know how to swim!
How can we know how our children will turn out?

A devout man lost his young son – trapped in a fire while
    rescuing others.
The man wept as he followed the casket to the grave, but
    he also danced.
Tears, yes, but why dancing? asked a friend.
Because a pure soul was lent to me, a pure soul I return.

Nothing so whole as a broken heart.

***

An old man in an old century remembered: *As long as there were no roads,*
and wolves roamed the forest, you had to interrupt a journey at nightfall.
Then you had all the leisure in the world to recite Psalms at the inn, open a book,
have a good talk. Nowadays, you can ride these roads day and night,
and there is no peace any more.

An old man in a new century remembers: *As long as there was no Facebook*
or Instagram, no Flickr or Twitter, no private music listened through ear buds –
then you had the leisure to recite poetry, meet friends at the pub, open a book,
have good talks with neighbours, family. Nowadays, you're ridden bareback
by these doodads, all day, all night. There is no peace any more.

***

Rebbe Levi-Yitzhak of Berditchev asked, why do books of knowledge begin on the second page? Because, however much one may learn, a person should always remember they've not even reached the beginning.

Why is food so expensive? Because people want to eat all the time.
If everyone wanted to learn all the time, learning would be expensive, food would be cheap.

To be religious is to worry not about what goes into your
    mouth,
but what comes out.

They tell of the poor man who couldn't read, but knew the
    letters
by heart. On Yom Kippur, instead of *shul*, he walked out
    in a field
reciting the *aleph bes*, one by one, asking God to form the
    prayer.

Caught me being frivolous or gossiping, my mother
    warned:
at birth we are each assigned a certain number of words.
Once the store runs out, we die.

Silence is a route to prolonged life.
Silence is the loudest sound of poetry.
Silence commemorates the six million.

***

The difference between a Rebbe and an ordinary rabbi:
A young person came to a rabbi and asked, *Is there a
    heaven?*
The rabbi consulted the Talmud: this one taught this, that
    one taught that.
And he consulted the Kabbalah, and he consulted the
    Shulchan Aruch,
and after some hours he ruled, *Yes, but only when the
    Messiah comes.*

The young person then went to a Rebbe and asked, *Is there
    a heaven?*
The Rebbe replied, *Yes, but don't wait until then.*

The rabbi answered the question. The Rebbe answered the person.

***

A Rebbe and his young disciple were on pilgrimage to a revered Tsaddik's tomb when they came upon a stream in spate. Near them was a young woman in long dress and head scarf – distressed, afraid to chance the crossing. The Rebbe lifted her gently onto his back, strode into the stream up to his waist, and crossed, the disciple following.

Once on the other side, the men walked silently for a long while until the disciple said, *Master, pardon me, but you shouldn't have touched that woman.* The Rebbe thought a moment, and replied, *I put her down some time ago. Why are you still carrying her?*

***

In every generation are thirty-six ordinary people,
the hidden righteous ones, doing ordinary deeds.
Among them: porters, teachers, sweepers,
carers, aunties and grannies who look after orphans.
They are God's emissaries. No one knows
who among us are elect, therefore we must honour all.

Pay attention to people on their way up, they will soon forget.
Pay attention to those on their way down, they will always remember.

Menachem Mendel of Rimanov taught
that welcoming guests is a greater virtue
than welcoming the Divine Presence.
When Abraham received angels he saw only
three dusty travellers who were famished, thirsting,
in need of rest.

But when Lot welcomed angels he already knew who they
     were.
Lot came to no good end: His daughters got him drunk
and slept with him to have his issue.

***

The words of Jewish prayer incessantly praising God bore
     me.
But I shouldn't listen to myself praying.
The moment I hear what I'm saying, I must
stop. Prayer isn't about you or me, not even about God;
     instead,
a form of humility, an interior hum. Pray with your body:
forwards, sideways, bent over. Sing. Loudly.

A Jew stranded on a desert island builds not one but two
     synagogues, because
I wouldn't be caught dead in that other one! The great
Tzadik Elimelekh once said: *Why are you surprised we
argue so much? This has always gone on between the
people of Israel. Alas for our souls! If this were not so, no
nation in the whole world could subjugate us.*

They tell this story of the Baal Shem Tov+: Some calamity
was facing the Jews.
(When aren't Jews faced with calamities?)
And so he went into the forest, lit a special fire, said a
special prayer,
and the disaster was averted. Decades later, another
catastrophe was on the way,
but we had forgotten how to make that fire. Yet, the prayer
still worked.
Generations later, we forgot the words to that prayer, but
we still remembered this story, which sufficed. But
now, after what happened to us, we're frantically trying to
re-tell the story.

We search fruitlessly for the 'X' that marks the treasure of
salvation. But the 'X' is always under our feet! When I go
to heaven they will not ask me why wasn't I the Baal Shem
Tov. They will ask me why wasn't I Norbert.

*Adaptations from Martin Buber's *Tales of the Hasidim*,
Elie Wiesel's *Souls on Fire*, and *Somewhere – A Master*;
and other sources.

+ Rabbi Israel ben Eliezer, known as the Baal Shem Tov,
'Master of the Good Name' (ca.1700-1760), founder of
Hasidism.

Outrageous, Strange

Each morning, but still a surprise:
a patch of light on the shoulder
of *Jabal Kanissa* enlarges,
spills down the slope, anointing
treetops, a far ridge, its village.

An amber glow glides into
the valley and mist-shrouded
hollows, last to come alive.

Each evening, but still a surprise:
a luciferous globe draws near
that thin line parting firmament
from water, world above from world below.
Its blinding light tempers – orange to red –
welcoming my gaze as it slips into the sea.

Outrageous, strange that I am given life
between one darkness and another darkness.

ACKNOWLEDGEMENTS

I am grateful to the editors of the following journals for publication of poems, some in earlier versions.

Acumen: *The Poet Fantasises,*

Fenland Reed: *Interrupted Journey, Lamentations*

Brittle Star: *A Nation Sundered*

Horror Zine: *Life-Course Department Store, Cat Meets Rat in New York Alley*

Hippocrates Press Competition Commendation: *Even If He Can't Answer Maybe He Can Hear You*

Hippocrates Press, anthology, 'Book of the Heart': *Heart Sounds*

Jewish Quarterly: *Shmita*

Locomotive: *Beirut Aubade*

London Grip: *The Disappeared, Repair Begins with Confusion, London Winter Blues*

Magma Competition Commendation: *On Reaching Seventy-Five*

Magma: *Killers Live Long, After the Barrel Bomb, The Penitent* (also in the anthology, "The Poet's Quest for God, Eyewear Publishing, as Avinu Malkeynu)

Poems for a Liminal Age, anthology, SPM Publications: *Syria 2017*

81

Poetry Salzburg Review: *Lebanon Mon Amour, The Pigeon Chaser*

Pulse: *My Friend the Scholar Comes at Last to Attend His Father*

Rising: *English Cuisine*

Salmagundi: *Three Score and Ten*

South Bank Poetry: *Letters from Vienna*

Templar Poetry Peloton Anthology: *Ode to My Old Passport Wallet*

The Ekphrastic Review: *Salomé With the Head of St. John The Baptist*

The Wolf: *Canon Lens 18-300 mm*

Earlier versions of *Self Portrait, Because It Is My Heart...*, were published in *A Cracked River* by Norbert Hirschhorn, Slow Dancer Poetry, 1999.

The Destined One was published under the title *Basherte* in *To Sing Away the Darkest Days* by Norbert Hirschhorn, Holland Park Press, 2013.

My heartfelt thanks go to Jacqueline Saphra for her close reading of the manuscript in draft. My poet colleagues at King's Poets, Highgate Poets and Torriano Workshop have helped make many of the poems much better. Cynthia Myntti keeps me happy and my poetry honest. My dear friend Fouad M. Fouad has given gracious permission to include the translations of his poems, which we worked on together.

AUTHOR

Norbert Hirschhorn is a physician specialising in international public health, commended in 1993 by President Bill Clinton as an *American Health Hero,* and following humbly in the tradition of physician-poets. He now lives in London. His poems have been published in over three dozen journals, and four full collections. Hirschhorn's work has won a number of prizes in the US and UK. More information is available from his website, www.bertzpoet.com.

Previous collections by Norbert Hirschhorn:

> *A Cracked River,* Slow Dancer Poetry, 1999
> *Mourning in the Presence of a Corpse,* Dar al-Jadeed, 2008
> *Monastery of the Moon,* Dar al-Jadeed, 2012
> *To Sing Away the Darkest Days – Poems Re-imagined from Yiddish Folk Songs,* Holland Park Press, 2013

Translated Author

Fouad M. Fouad is also a physician and poet. He comes from Aleppo. Following the outbreak of the war in Syria he and his family moved to Lebanon where he is now at the American University of Beirut. Dr Fouad is deeply engaged in research and action on behalf of Syrian refugees. He has published five volumes of poetry in Arabic; the latest called, *Once Upon a Time in Aleppo*. Several of his poems have appeared in translation in English and French poetry journals.

Holland Park Press is a unique publishing initiative. Its aim is to promote poetry and literary fiction, and discover new writers. It specializes in contemporary English fiction and poetry, and translations of Dutch classics. It also gives contemporary Dutch writers the opportunity to be published in Dutch and English. .

To

- Learn more about Norbert Hirschhorn
- Discover other interesting books
- Read our unique Anglo-Dutch magazine
- Find out how to submit your manuscript
- Take part in one of our competitions

Visit www.hollandparkpress.co.uk

Bookshop: https://www.hollandparkpress.co.uk/books.php

Holland Park Press in the social media:

http://www.twitter.com/HollandParkPres
http://www.facebook.com/HollandParkPress
https://www.linkedin.com/company/holland-park-press
http://www.youtube.com/user/HollandParkPress